C000143004

SILENTLY WITHIN
MODERN SUFI POETRY

SILENTLY WITHIN

MODERN SUFI POETRY

DEBORAH O'BRIEN BELL

PARAS

1996

Published by
PARAS
BM BOX 6596
London WC1N 3XX

Cover and book design,
ornament and illustrations
by © Deborah O'Brien Bell

Set in Times by Evergreen Design, London.
Japanese translation by Guhen Kitaoka

Printed and bound in Ireland by
O'Brien Printing
Barrow Street, Dublin 4.

British Library Cataloguing in Publication Data
    Bell, Deborah, 1946
    Silently Within:
    Modern Sufi poetry
    1. Sufi poetry, English — 20th century
    2. English poetry — 20th century.
    1. Title
    821.9'14
ISBN 1 874292 26 4

Dedicated to my children,
Sonia, Shikha and Christopher
and to all children
of now and the future;
this new time, this new beginning,
is for you.

Life

Into my life you came like a storm of monsoon
banging down like an eastern sky.
And you scattered me, like the wind disperses
dry grass and the petals of flowers.
Out of myself You scattered me into Nothingness
Beyond the Nowhere, beyond the Beyond.

IRENA TWEEDIE.

Silence

CONTENTS

Contents

Contents

If ten men want to enter a house,
and only nine find their way in,
the tenth must not say:
This is what God ordained.
He must find out what
his own shortcoming was.

RUMI

Soul

FOREWORD

In the writing of these verses I am helped to ground some understanding of my experiences. They may mirror your experiences and your understandings, the substance may be the same. If these outpourings resonate with you, then it is a beautiful thing that we meet and are one voice.

Deborah O'Brien Bell

In the pursuit of learning one knows more each day;
in the pursuit of The Way one knows less each day.
One knows less and less until one knows nothing at all,
and when one does nothing at all, there is nothing that is undone.

Lao Tzu

Silently within
passion extinguishes itself
the dance dissolves
the honeymoon is over,
and that space
that space which is between lovers,
remains.

Heart

The human heart
is limitless,
for it forms part
of the Great Heart.

·BHAI SAHIB

At Your bequest a pilgrimage
dwells in the hearts of man.
It is a quest of many names and guises
and asks of all to seek the hidden treasure.
It seeks in those lost in mists
and calls to those asleep in dreams
it pursues the many who never rest
in their conquests of the earth.
For You, who bestowed this pilgrimage,
who created all the days and nights,
who wrote the dharma,
You are the servant who serves His creation.
We can but ask of You, to show your grace,
to shine your light, to let be known
the all that is within,
to tear apart the countless veils
that hide the sacred treasure,
to know the truth, to realize the real,
to know the false

so all the shadows of the mind are seen,
let us serve You.
In your infinite compassion
You prompt the winds of changing direction
to move in those who have lost
their sense of You, who journey
in the wilderness of time. You knock
on the doors of those hearts ceaselessly,
You shake the foundations of certainty and
press to bend to render soft all hardness.
All this you do for your love of Man
so he can know You and You serve him.
The warriors of the inner skies in their
seekings to find the precious jewel,
they see the endlessness of birth and death
and take up battle to slay the dragon
and cut the samsara.
In that doing they clean the mirror
of all that gatherers on the line of man.

They learn ceasing to make another link
that joins the past to the past
and the past to the present
and the present to the future.
In that there forms a link with
all eternity with those who went before
and showed the way,
they are the sweepers and the gatherers,
and they serve You.
To some you give the fire of light
and ears to hear what God alone does speak,
they journey on alone and walk
the silent path that very few do seek,
they leave the darkened passages
and climb the highest peaks.
They are the servants and they serve You.
For You are the guide and sage of all
creator of the created and un manifest.
It is Your gift that this pilgrimage
dwells in the hearts of man.

The mirror and the mirrored
the reflection and the gaze
the looking and the seeing
two images
two way glances,
seeing that which is you
is also me too,
seeing that which is me
is also you too,
the you in me
the me in you.

受容性

Receptivity

The principle thing
is the receptivity of the soul.

RUMI

This shattered heart
I give to You.
Please take it
for it carries too many memories,
please take it
for no crack can mend
no piece made new
no more can it do,
it is shattered.
Please take it to the fire
that burns all to dust.
Grant me a heart,
a heart that is new,
a heart born of love,
the love that is You.

Just like that!
a full stop,
and every cell of me knew
that there was no point any more -
no reference point,
no road
no path
no teacher,
no anything to hold onto
simply nothing anymore.
And out of this full stop,
this ceasing,
became the point of stillness,
of being this very moment,
being no where else
but here.

You my soul who cries in the night
sees the ripening bough
and the golden fruit.
You know that there is no other god
but He who turns the days and nights.
And in your longing and sorrowing
you cry to this nothing
to be the quantum leap of flowing
in Infinite space and Knowledge.

When looking for the eternal friend
look not to the outer world,
for none can be that but Him alone.
He the Beloved One is the friend -
eternal and forever.
He comes silently
into the longings of the heart
like a gentle breeze on a summer night.
And on those windy days
when all hopes fade away
and standing naked in grief or sorrow
He is there in His love and His compassion,
and He will enfold you
and He will hold you
and He will carry you.
For He is the lover of lovers
and guide of all.
He comes into the heart of the one
who longs for him.

Beyond

How can the mind
understand
that which is beyond
the mind.

KRISTNAMURTI

I am at a cross roads with no sign posts.
All stands still
and the deadening hollowness cuts.
A whirl pool of thoughts
sucks me into confusion
and I am caught in worlds
of dreams and imaginings.
I want to fill this space,
this empty empty space
with what to do, where to go,
how to be, how to see.
If I could hold this emptiness,
if I could let it hold me,
let the dust settle and see
that I am sitting
in the doorway of nothingness,
where I can but wait and be.

Great Teachers tell us
that we are the weavers of our realities.
That we spin each day to each day
into shapes of sameness
into patterns of endless repetitions.
With each face the play is the same played
over and over again.
From the source that is us
comes the same recipe
the same ingredients
the same flavour
the same taste.

Inside is the dance of lovers
and the ecstasy of union,
and That which stirs this dance
is the constant pulse that
stirs the heart of all creation.
For within this dance
this dance of lovers,
there is the birthless birth
the wordless song of knowninglessness,
there the heart turns and turns
to the constant spinning
of the mystic journey home.

Sinking, sinking, sinking,
sinking through the passage of my pain
I found me longing for You.
Sinking, sinking, sinking,
sinking into the bottomless,
the pit of my pain
I found You longing for me.
I had thought that You were outside of me
far away, somewhere else, where I called
and called and longed for You, where You
called and called and longed for me.
Sinking, sinking, sinking
sinking into the core of my pain
I find You longing for me
longing for You longing for me
longing for You longing for me,
and in this dance
You and me so intertwined -
one pain,
one longing.

Infinite

He is infinite,
there is an infinite variety
of conceptions of Him
and endless variety of paths to Him.

ANANDAMAYI MA

In praise of Him who is not,
in praise of That that is,
bowing down to all that is nothing
deep deep stillness moves
and like the wind moves You move.
And I praise the ways
that are of beyond all matter and form.
And as the sun shines
You shine
embracing all.
And as the birds fly
so do I with You.

Listen.....
the silence is heard above the crowd
above the sound of traffic,
and those Great Ones that went before
beckon us with the
sweetness of that song.
They call us with the smile of the heart
and showers of bitter sweet longing.
The door is always open,
and waiting at the threshold they stand
with open hands outstretched before us.

Pain is His gift to show
what lurks in the shadows,
memories of yesterday
hurts of the past,
pain of a loss
pain of a cross,
pain of a need
disappointment, a sorrow.
Pain is His gift
so we can know all of ourselves.
Pain is His love
His helping us see,
so that we can be free.

How can what we see last forever
does not youthful hair turn grey ?
we all turn to dust someday.
Never turn away from the love within
it is a cave of hidden treasure,
rarest gems,
it has no measure.

沈

默

Silence

Hammer your head
into your heart
and think from there.

SUFI SAYING

The relationship with the mystery
is such a thing to allow,
for great courage is needed and great faith.
What is asked is that you surrender yourself
totally into the hands of the Friend of God,
this Friend who given golden threads to weave
will take you safely deeply
into the innermost core of being
where the very private and intimate
love affair with the mystery takes place.

Before time my name was called
and the echo echoed.
O I knew that one step on this road
would close the doors to going back
to the ways of my fathers fathers.
and my mothers mothers.
On this solitary quest
I cried till all the earth was wet.
To the winds and the moons I cried,
O come and enfold me, enfold me in That
which sweeps away the shadows
that quenches my thirst.
O beloved ocean of understanding
O crescent new moon
O city of my Teacher who held me,
who built a pyre that raged
and rendered the way of dust.
Was it all the pain of my illusions
that swept my earthly floor,
was it more than that that hurled and swirled
endless hurricanes within my heart,
that left me naked, utterly alone.

Devotion is a woman saturated in waiting
surrendered in love.
Like the dawn her silence
permeates every new day
and as she dances she is heard
to sing a thousand thanks
to sigh a thousand sighs.
Like a dew drop glistening
she waits to be dissolved.
She is a flower opening to the light
and calls in gentle whispers -
O bow down,
surrender yourself,
hear the song of the Blessed One.

Sitting -
A silence night
pregnant with unendingness,
a melody of emptiness
a chorus of heaven on earth
and the divine heart of eternity.

Rising in love
soaring in eternity
held in That which some call God.
Held in That heart
and in That hand is held the mystery
of the sublime unveiling itself
of loves luminous song
of love naked in aloneness.
O my heart you heard the call,
and O my heart you dared to answer.

God

God is with those
who patiently persevere.

KORAN

I cannot stop the tides from turning
coming in to reach the shore,
I cannot stop the moon from rising
reflecting light,
exposing more.
I cannot stop my heart from opening
touched by love by fire and grace,
I cannot stop my heart from melting
turning, turning
empty space.

My teacher set me afire
to the way of the heart
sat me amongst people of the path
keepers of golden fruits.
My teacher set me aflame.
to fire catching the wind
burning burning
rendering down
returning.

When the heart is hard there is no love
in the house no sap to bend the tree
no song to greet the rising sun
no dance, not free.
Like a shrivelled hardened nut
it hides within its shell
it knows no overflow
it feels like hell.
But life in all its compassion knows
it will have to fashion mighty blows
to crack, to shatter open,
to bring into the light this heart.
In these awakening moments
rivers of tears are cried
and hours of pain felt,
very delicate moments
regaining a vulnerable state.
A softened heart bathed in tears
knows the enfoldment of the love of All love
and no longer needs to hide.

It is a freedom song -
this being here to go beyond
all that is of the emotions and the mind,
beyond all that binds us to
the endless personality of the ego.
This being here to go beyond
all that we are conditioned to do and think,
is a freedom song
so bitter sweet.

神秘家

Mystic

The mystic hears
a different drummer.

AYYA KHEMA

You gave me a longing in my heart
and left me baying at the moon,
this longing became my days and nights.
You gave me a longing in my heart
and left me bare to wear a crown of thorns
to walk my days like a ghost at dusk.
You crushed my dreams
scattered them like ashes
surrendered me prostrate to the ground.
You took me to Yourself,
You took my pain
showed me the way of no return
of bending
moving with the wind.
Set aflame
burnt inside out
ashes to ashes
dust to dust.

I am waiting,
waiting as a woman waits for her lover.
There is no question, there is no doubt.
With all my heart I know that I am loved.
This state of waiting, waiting to dissolve,
to dissolve in That, my love,
is a precious time.
For when my Beloved comes
descending like mist in silence
there are no footsteps
there are no sounds
His presence surrounds,
where I am He is.

Let me sing a thousand songs
let them be all of You,
let my voice be the song of songs -
divine and true.
Let me dance the dance of Siva
that is beyond the rhythm of time,
let me die into the mystery -
that is You.

I am indeed grateful to That
which is an unsolvable equation,
abstract,
beyond any time
beyond any thought
beyond any form.
I call That my Beloved,
I am a Sufi,
it is one spiritual form,
one way of being
that is All.

There is no moment but now.
Yesterday is but a memory
and tomorrow
a mere possibility.

最も甘い

Most sweet

Your name
on my tongue
is the sweetest word.

RABI'A.

Setting sun
misty mountains
pines mighty and high,
the scent of eucalyptus flowers
lifts me,
I dance,
the moon is in the sky
clouds turn pink
then to grey.
Today I am filled
with the song of gratitude -
time to pray.

Moon lake, your Gaelic name Loughloon,
so named because your waters
take the splendour of the moon,
and all the troubles of the world away
as shining night descends like day.
Quiescence and the dreamer meet
and play a dance -
a melody of silent awe and wonder,
and the child in me delights to see the sea
as lake of silver shines.
Opened wide my heart breaths in
my soul my spirit can not hide
for all around is drenched in love,
and I stay and drink the wine.

For Eireen
Loughloon is a town land in West Clare,Ireland.

It was Doolin and the sky was grey
it was more than surf
that crashed high that day -
it was might, it was white,
it was a sight to bring
a soul to humble watching.
The winds wild I was a child
framing fragments with a camera.
On another day when the sun was shining
the waters hardly moved,
the slucán was harvesting
and walking felt I a soft warm breeze,
O the blue of the sky and the warmth of the sun
and the hawthorn naked in the fields -
then echoes of a winter night

a thistle still frosted -
a crystal prince sparkled light
a wondrous sight,
the tranquillity of that day,
what could I say!,
an inward voice prayed a thankful thanks.
Then a quote of note
came to my head, which said -

  'What is this life if full of care
   we have no time to stand and stare
   no time to stand beneath the bows
   to stare as long as sheep or cows.'

*Quote by W.H.Davies.
*Slucán is a winter seaweed
*Doolin is a town land in West Clare,Ireland.

The orange beak
of a lone bird shines bright,
a branch covered with buds
makes a fine perch.
A warmness arises
when I see the first blossom
white on the tree
and in the moonlight
they are a delight.
On the last day of Spring,
I see a honey bee
going from blossom to blossom.
while a gentle wind
takes them falling
like snow to the ground.

All are looking for love,
some glimpse it looking at the stars
others while writing songs,
a mother while holding child to breast
fishermen while rolling in full nets,
craftsmen while shaping wood, silver, gold,
children while playing in street or field,
all are looking for love.
Lovers glimpse it in a sweet embrace,
the farmer while tilling soil,
the nurse while caring for the sick,
all are looking for love.
But all these experiences
they come and they go,
they are the tides of life helping us
to know that these experiences are reflections
of the love that is always there.

The tree cut at the roots
controlled and conditioned not to grow
never to reach its full potential
to dance its greatest dance.
Never to have birds nesting
and singing in its branches,
never to have people resting in its shade,
O, the bonsai tree.

意識

Consciousness

Consciousness is born
with the pain of separation.

LLEWELLYN VAUGHAN LEE

You pointed to the way of no return
tore up the map I cherished,
scattered it piece by piece to the winds
I was shattered.
With love you led me to the fires
few words, so much compassion.
This journey of no return truly means
there is no going back to old ways.
Bridges burning -
set aflame by my beloved teacher
who is with me now,
who is my heart
who is my transgression.

Power

Life is the power
of God alone.

YUNUS EMRE

The ego wants the glory
of the manifest and unseen -
wants the very place where I stand.
wants to be bigger than itself.
And like with a child
I hold its hand
befriend it with my heart -
then its desire sits quietly.

Tell me, who really wants the Truth ?,
people run at the mere utterance of its name.
But Truth never ceases calling us,
it whispers and talks to all hearts
and comes as a sword to many.
Mercy is not its name and it, a shape shifter
adapts to our time and place.
Truth brings blessings in disguise and in
compassion waits till we see the face
that wants to be seen.
I have run from the truth of who I am
and tried to loosen the grip of its holding
me to standing still, to seeing all of my faces.
My teacher taught me to stand before that mirror,
to bear the pain of my delusions and of the
not wanting to face the face I saw before me.
To be and see the truth of who I am,
to embrace it, is easier said than done,
and is done easier and easier,
and one day by the grace of god
let me see the mirror clean.

I became that tear drop
that moved the land to cry
and the moon to fade away.
Then You called you did,
You ordered the severity of Love to walk in
and all hell inside broke out
and the tables turned upside down
and I stood trembling,
and against my will
bowed down to let humility in -
that was the task at hand
to crush the hardened shell
of my resisting will.
You showered rays of sun
between those thundering skies .
to let my mind be still and emotions rest.
The outcome that Your asked for, was,
that the longing to see Your face
became that burning flame
through which You entered in.

Held in the heart of all creation
the Sufi heart is filled with love,
filled with the mystery of it.
Wedded to the Beloved one
forever in His embrace,
the Sufi heart is soft
vulnerable in the mystic sense.
Knowing His love is the love of all love,
the Sufi heart beats to the rhythm of His name
and sings the song that praises Him alone.
Held in the heart of the heart of all hearts,
the Sufi heart rests in That alone.

Swimming against the flow
sometimes one just cannot move
against the strength of it.
And sometimes when nearly sinking
prayer can be forgotten
and the effort of keeping afloat
plays a harrowing note,
and as the waters cover the face
the compass says there is
no other way to go, but up stream
no other way to go, but up stream.

Divine

The divine life
is the most fulfilling
and natural way
of life on earth.

BARRY LONG

Which ever teacher calls
go
for that teacher
is life itself calling you.
It is life knowing
the recesses of your heart
the music and dance of your spirit
and the needs and longings of your soul.
Which ever teacher calls
go
for your spirit and soul know
the sound of that calling.

Fragile moments,
on the edge of a precipice
emerges moments being born
into what I do not know -
and the nothingness of that
seems like I am an illusion,
no substance anymore,
just fragile moments on the edge
drinking from the cup of surrender
and the sweetness of That elixir
is like wild mountain honey.

Forever

So let us be pure, ringing notes,
never out of tune,
singing His praise forever

IRENA TWEEDIE

Great are the traditions
of the unseen, the unspoken,
for they weave time to time
bind man to heart and soul.
Great are the traditions
that mark the journey Home.
Threads, golden threads,
ancient blessedness,
ancient knowingness,
eternity bestowed.

Ride through the storm
for it can only wet you,
ride fast, ride firm
for it can only hurl around you,
steadily ride, one pointed direction.
And if you should fall,
sink in the mud,
find difficulty mounting to ride on again,
pray to be steadfast, not lost in defeat
for this is a time of reflection.

Let us make a bridge,
a bridge between worlds,
so that which is in separation
is dissolved into One.

ACKNOWLEDGEMENTS

I wish to thank my brother Dermot for his very generous assistance with the printing of this volume.

For permission to use copyrighted material, I wish to acknowledge: The Golden Sufi Centre, PO Box 428, Inverness, CA 94937, USA, for permission to quote from Daughter of Fire by Irena Tweedie and In the Company of Friends by LLewellyn Vaughan Lee; The Barry Long Foundation BCM Box, London WC1N 3XX, UK, for permission to quote from Barry Long's Journal, Number One; Penguin Group Ltd.,London, for permission to quote Ayya Khema and Anandamayi Ma, 25 words (p68 & p116) from Weavers of Wisdom, Women Mystics of the Twentieth Century (Arkana 1989) © Anne Bancroft, 45 words (p109) from Tao Te Ching by Lao Tzu, translation by D.C.Lau (Penguin Classics 1963) © D.C.Lau; Threshold Books, 139 Main St. Brattleboro, Vt.05301 USA, for permission to quote from Door Keepers of the Heart, Versions of Rabi'a, translated by Charles Upton and Signs of the Unseen, Discourses of Jalaluddin Rumi, translated by W.M.Thackston, Jr.; The author would like to acknowledge gratitude to quote from Yunus Emre, The Wondering Fool translated by Edouard Roditi, published by Cadmus Editions, San Francisco, USA.
Photograph by Niravi Ahrenhold

Deborah O'Brien Bell was born in Dublin, Ireland in 1946. She was educated there at the National College of Art & Design. In 1986 she moved to London. Six months later she started to sit with Irena Tweedie of the Naqshbandiyya-Mujaddidiyya Order of Sufism. They are known as the Golden Sufis, the Silent Sufis. Since then Deborah has been guided by this line and tradition. She knows that to be a Sufi is more than a way of life, it is to be embraced by the very Heart of the universe. The Sufi way is referred to as *The Way of the Heart,* they are also known as *The People of the Path* and *The Lovers and Friends of God.* Deborah lives as a craftsperson in North London, occasionally giving readings from the Mystics and her own work. She has three children, two daughters and a son.

We go to the Absolute Truth in silence,
for it can be found only in silence, and it is Silence.
That is why we are called the Silent Sufis.
        IRENA TWEEDIE

Path